May God bless you in your finances with His freedom!

Love,
Charity

PERSONAL FINANCES

PERSONAL FREEDOM

Chanty Webb

Published by
Olive Press צהר זית
Messianic and Christian Publisher
P.O. Box 163
Copenhagen, NY 13626

Our prayer at Olive Press is that we may help make the Word of Adonai fully known, that it spread rapidly and be glorified everywhere. We hope our books help open people's eyes so they will turn from darkness to Light and from the power of the adversary to God and to trust in ישוע Yeshua (Jesus). (From II Thess. 3:1; Col. 1:25; Acts 26:18,15 NRSV and CJB, the *Complete Jewish Bible*)
May this book in particular help people everywhere find financial freedom.

In honor to God, pronouns referring to the Trinity are capitalized. But not all Bible versions do this and legally must be printed as they are.

www.olivepresspublisher.com

Cover photo and design © 2013 by Randi J. Dean. www.randijdean.com
Author photo © 2013 by Lisa Q. Shay
Interior design © 2013 by Olive Press

PERSONAL FINANCES PERSONAL FREEDOM

Copyright © 2013 by Chanty Webb

All rights reserved. No part of this book may be reproduced, stored in a retrieval system, or transmitted in any way by any means—electronic, mechanical, photocopy, recording, or otherwise—without the prior permission of the copyright holder, except as provided by USA copyright law.

ISBN 978-0-9847111-7-8
Printed in the USA.

1. Personal Finances 2. Autobiography 3. Christian Inspirational

Unless otherwise noted, all Scripture quotations are taken from the *Holy Bible, New International Version.* Copyright © 1973, 1978, 1984 by International Bible Society. All rights reserved.

Scripture quotations marked HCSB are taken from the Holman Christian Standard Bible®, Copyright © 1999, 2000, 2002, 2003 by Holman Bible Publishers. Used by permission. Holman Christian Standard Bible®, Holman CSB®, and HCSB® are federally registered trademarks of Holman Bible Publishers.

This book is dedicated
to my mom, Mary Ruth,
who planted the first seeds
of my faith in God.

WITH SPECIAL THANKS

The glory goes to my Heavenly Father for anything that you may glean from this book. It was His Holy Spirit that wrote the script, and His determined Son, Jesus, who died to give me abundant life. Everything in this book that makes you laugh, that makes you cry, that makes you nod your head in understanding is because God allowed me to suffer through some things only to come out stronger and wiser on the other side. When I find out about a good deal, I have to share it with somebody. In the same way, God has used this book to share His goodness with others. HE is the REAL DEAL!

My husband, Ross, is the best—best friend, best lover, best counselor, and best dad. He has a brilliant mind and I am privileged to reap the benefits of his brilliance. Thank you, Honey, for your love and support as I become the woman that God wants me to be.

Morgan, Hunter, and Blaise, I am privileged to be your mom. Believe me when I say that I love you even when you don't see a smile on my face. Thank you for making me look like the best mom in the world.

Mom, I thank you for your sacrifice. It was not easy for you to take three girls and venture out on your own. But you always told us that God would provide and you were always right. I remember money coming out of nowhere for groceries that we needed. You planted those first seeds of my belief in God and I love you for it.

Dad, thank you for showing me the benefits of hard work. I didn't understand it as a child, but now I appreciate the discipline that it has taught me. I love you.

Cheryl and Chawanna, thank you both for reading my book, giving me input, and applying what you learned. It is such a compliment to have your support and your love.

Pastor, you are my Dream Coach. You have taught me so much. One lesson that I will carry with me is that my confidence is not in who I am but in who God is. I praise the Lord for you having lived.

Audree, you have shown me the strength that comes with waiting on God. Your life models what you preach. I admire your faith in the promises of God.

Joyce Davis, I have been blessed in being one of the first fruits of your author's ministry. Thank you for sharing your talent and time.

Stephanie Richardson, you must know that I appreciate your first edits of my manuscript. In the midst of participating in so many projects, you took the time to also serve me. Not that this comes as a surprise.

A special thank you to all those who have discipled me in order to help me grow, as well as those who have allowed me to disciple them in their growth. God has used you to sharpen me so that I can become more like His Son, Jesus.

CONTENTS

FOREWORD	10
INTRODUCTION: ARE YOU READY?	13
1. GROWING UP	15
2. THE COLLEGE YEARS	23
3. WORKING WOMAN	31
4. THE TWO (DEBTS) SHALL BECOME ONE (BIG DEBT)	35
5. AFTER THE HONEYMOON	43
6. THE TURNING POINT	55
7. READING, WRITING, AND ARITHMETIC	61
8. PUTTING IT INTO PRACTICE	65
9. DEBT DEMOLITION	75
10. BUYING AND BLESSING	93
11. PASSING IT ON	99
EPILOGUE: PERSONAL FREEDOM	109
RECOMMENDED READING	111

FOREWORD

After spending twenty plus years in senior management with Fortune 100 Companies along with twenty years as a senior pastor helping God's people to understand and apply His word, I have found that there is a serious lack of commitment to money management. Biblical financial principles guarantee success—period. The devastation that occurs when the tail wags the dog can be life-dominating. America is said to be on the "cliff" financially. Unfortunately, families are a microcosm of the condition of this nation.

I married Ross and Chanty thirteen years ago. For years they silently struggled with their personal finances. One day they made the decision to put their hand to the plow and demolish their debt. Over the next couple of years following that decision, they reaped the benefits of their labor—breaking free of $44,000 worth of debt! Since that time, they have committed to teaching others how to better manage their personal finances. This commitment to help others gave birth to Chanty's book, *Personal Finances Personal Freedom*.

After picking up Chanty's manuscript, it was difficult to put down. The transparency of her story is relative to many of us and shows Biblical truths in action. It is plain to see how anyone who commits to reading this book and applying its principles can also experience financial freedom. While this book was penned by a woman, men will find it easy to read and most certainly relate to Ross' plight of carrying the financial burden as the head of his home.

Personal Finances Personal Freedom is a must-read for anyone desiring to create order out of financial chaos. As a certified Biblical counselor, I look forward to using Chanty's book both to prepare couples for marriage as well as to provide hope for married couples wrestling with financial hardship. Don't miss out! As the Webb's Pastor, I am honored to see them pursuing their dream. Chanty is like the character "Champion" in Bruce Wilkinson's *The Dream Giver*. She was a Nobody, who became a Somebody, and can now help Anybody. If you are ready to be purposeful with your money and experience abundant living (John 10:10b), I charge you to get this book and read on!

Dr. Clifford Ashe III
Senior Pastor and Founder of DaySpring Ministries
CEO Mighty Men of Valor

INTRODUCTION

Are you ready?

It has been said that until the pain of staying the same is greater than the pain of change, you will not change. I write this book because God has given me freedom from financial debt. Are you ready to be free?

You think, "Of course I'm ready. Who doesn't want to be out of debt?" Well, are you ready to give up (temporarily or permanently) having your nails done? Dining out? Impulse shopping? Extravagant gifting? Lottery tickets? Buying the neighbor kid's Girl Scout cookies? Weekly golf with the guys?

Is it painful yet?

December 26, 2008 is the date my husband and I became consumer debt free after nine years of marriage. Time and again we had talked about getting our finances in order. But it was not until August 2006 that we began doing the work required to bring about this order. Why did we wait? The answer is simple. We were not in enough pain. Still content to charge vacations and spend impulsively, we felt it would be more painful for us to give up these pleasures than to sacrifice them until a later time. Then one day we reached our breaking point—the day when our lack of responsibility impacted our children. That was the day we knew we had to change.

CHAPTER 1

GROWING UP

GROWING UP

I had it pretty good. My dad owned his own business and our family was well off—not rich—but comfortable. Our family of five (mom, dad and three girls) had the privilege of taking annual family trips, some of which involved air travel, not a cheap undertaking for a family our size. On holidays we would typically get a majority of the gifts we asked for.

That being said, we were not spoiled kids. My dad taught us the value of hard work. During the summers and any other days off from school, we were not in childcare. We were in dad's store doing inventory, steaming pants, running the register, and doing other age-appropriate work. As children we did not get an allowance. We received pay for work like the other employees. This concept was instilled in us at an early age, and I could not be more grateful. Of course at the time I did not appreciate it. But isn't that how we all are? The Bible says, No discipline seems pleasant at the time, but painful. Later on, however, it produces a harvest of righteousness and peace for those who have been trained by it (Hebrews 12:11). It was not fun being trained as a child in this manner (although I do have some great memories from it). However, it prepared me to accept the required discipline for becoming debt-free. God is indeed sovereign!

Another lesson we were taught is to value possessions—not necessarily the possessions themselves, but

Chapter 1 Growing up

the hard work required to obtain these possessions. I can recall repeatedly being lectured on the care of the "grown-up" record player every single time we kids used it. My dad was very protective when it came to material things in our home.

One incident I will never forget. My younger sister and I (always partners in crime) were playing in the living room. We were probably about 7 and 9 years old, respectively. Dad had recently purchased a ceramic tiger that was about three feet tall. Being kids with active imaginations, we had the brilliant idea of teaching the tiger to lie down and "play dead." We quickly learned that this tiger was 1) not designed to "play dead" and 2) much heavier than we thought. Down went the tiger and off rolled its head! We were devastated, not because our trick did not work, but because we knew a spanking would soon follow—and it did! This reinforced the point that we should not take possessions for granted. Today my children are taught that same respect and value for their own and other people's property.

As a child working at my dad's clothing store, I learned some of my first lessons about consumer debt. During that time in the early 80's, my dad made the decision to allow some of his customers to open a charge account at the store. This allowed select people to take home clothing without paying for it. I remember thinking about this concept as a luxury that special people were given. The people with these charge accounts were generally "good customers"—the regulars that he would see on a daily basis and did not think would leave him hanging with an unpaid bill. I did not associate anything bad with these people—in fact quite the opposite. In my eyes they were special people who received special privileges because of the consumer history they had with my dad's business. He allowed them to leave without paying for his merchandise because he trusted them to pay for it eventually and then purchase even more merchandise in the future!

I have heard it said that drug dealers will give their clients the first "hit" for free. Why? Because they know that once they have had it, they will be back. The person is thinking, "Wow, what a great guy! He treated me well and I didn't even have to pay for what I got. He just gave it to me!" Well, if you think about it, isn't credit the same way? You do not have to pay for a credit card account—not in the beginning. But in the end, just like with taking drugs, you end up paying more than what the merchandise was ever worth. I wish I would have been that perceptive at such an early age. But, alas, my understanding was that generally the people who got these accounts were model citizens.

Now on the flip side of that, I also saw the 30-, 60- and 90-day notices that we sent to the handful of people who did not pay on their accounts. Mailing out these notices of delinquency was one of my jobs. I knew the names well after several months of sending the same letters to the same people. I also knew that we would likely never see that money outside of taking some legal action. My dad, usually a good judge of

Chapter 1 Growing up

financial integrity, sometimes extended credit to people who were not credible. I would look at the names and hear how my dad talked about these people—in my mind they were bad people. Bad people because they would not pay their bills. Never did I stop to think that maybe they could not pay their bills.

When I was about 13 years old, my parents got a divorce. My mom, who had been employed with my dad's business for the majority of her married life, had to find work. Can you imagine losing your marriage and your job in the same space of time? Yes, divorce is rough on kids and was rough for us. But sometimes, I think the adults have it worst of all. Generally children get to see both parents and there still exists a love relationship between parent and child. The adult, however, loses a spouse, a friend, and a status (being married) all at the same time. Can you see why God hates divorce? (Malachi 2:16a) He hates seeing His children suffer.

Just the same, my mom found work and did what she needed to do to support three girls. She first ran a daycare from our home for a couple of years. This worked as she could be around for us, but unfortunately, it did not pay enough to make ends meet. My sisters and I continued to work at the clothing store and regularly contributed to the household finances. Most times kids will work or get an allowance to pay for the stuff that they want. But, we were working to pay for the stuff that we needed, like groceries, electricity, and water. The money we made was paying for our family to survive—quite a rude awakening at 13 years of age.

With money being tight, we moved out of our home where we had grown up and moved into a smaller house closer to the city. My father moved back into the home we left, re-married and continues to raise his family there to this day. He did pay child support and gave us money as we needed it. But it never seemed to be enough. I don't say this to discredit my dad—it's just one of the many downsides of divorce.

Although my father would pay child support and contribute to our living expenses, there were always unexpected expenses that would arise. No, I'm not talking about a pair of Jordache jeans. (I know, I'm taking you way back.) I'm talking about a hospitalization, a vehicle in need of repair—things that take you by surprise. And because that relationship was no longer there between my mother and father, my mom probably did not want to be in the position of asking Dad for more money and my dad probably did not trust that the money he was giving to Mom was being used in the proper manner. This left the situation of a stalemate, and the end result was us living hand to mouth. As the money came in, the money went out. This was not a smart situation to be in, but from what I knew we had no choice. My mom was the head of the household now and she did the best that she could. I do not know how she handled the bills exactly. All I know is that when my paycheck came in, I gave her the majority of it. It went towards our survival.

Chapter 1 Growing up

Boy, I resented that! Out of my resentment, I used the fact that I contributed money to the household to manipulate my mom's feelings about me. Now before I continue, I must let you know that I was a "good kid." I did not drink, smoke, or have sex in high school. I would go to parties but did none of the above at them. That was my definition of a good kid.

On one particular occasion I was going to get ice cream after my senior high awards ceremony. At that ceremony I had gotten a scholarship award to the tune of a $500 check. I had my mom's car and had not said anything to her about going out with friends after the ceremony. Well, I came home late that night and when I got in I could tell Mom was fuming. What was the first thing I said to her? "Hey, Mom, look what I got at the awards ceremony tonight!" I showed her the check and all was well.

Yes, I did know that it was wrong, but I also knew that it saved my butt and secured my future use of her vehicle! I saw the power that I had over my mom when I had money—dysfunctional, yes, but in my eyes, profitable. Although I did have this advantage in being a partial breadwinner, it was not worth it. I knew that the position that I held was not appropriate. A parent was supposed to hold that position. It made me feel uncomfortable, and in my view my mom was "lesser than" because she could not provide for us. My sisters and I had more financial responsibility than any child should ever have and it was a set-up for future financial failure.

Personal Finances Personal Freedom

CHAPTER 2

THE COLLEGE YEARS

Personal Finances Personal Freedom

AS I SHARED earlier, I was a good kid. I was close with other good kids and got good grades. These good grades helped get me into college. However, they didn't completely pay for it. Money was still an issue.

These days you hear a lot about parents setting up a 529 plan or ESA (Educational Savings Account) for their children, which allows for contributions to be made by loved ones towards the child's college education. In other words, the child's parents have not only thought about but have made plans to fund a college education. No such planning was done for me. My parents and I just did not think about it. Yes, I wanted to go to college. Yes, my parents wanted me to go to college. However, no premeditated process was in place to ensure that this would be possible.

I remember talking to my dad behind the register at his clothing store, trying to understand all of the paperwork behind acquiring a student loan. I knew that it meant I would have money to go to college. But I certainly did not realize the debt that I was about to be chained to for the next fifteen years!

You might ask, "What about scholarships?" Well, I did receive one scholarship from the university that paid $3000 per year for up to five years. I praise God because only He knew that I would be in school for an "extra" year! Unlike most scholarships, I did not have

Chapter 2 The College Years

to do anything for this one. They looked at my racial background, my grades, and poof! I got some money.

Unfortunately I had not planned ahead enough to actually apply for any other scholarships (foolish, yes, I know) and I was down to the wire in terms of deadlines. I needed the money now! So $15,000 in student loans (not including interest) was the route that I took to finance my future.

Now I must be perfectly honest in sharing with you that I did not connect with the fact that this money was my debt and my responsibility. At college they were required to show a presentation to everyone who received a student loan. The presentation emphasized paying it back after college. Aside from that point, I cannot remember much else.

I did not know about the interest that began after I graduated. I did not even know that you didn't have to accept the full amount that you were given if you didn't need it! "After I graduate" was a long time away, so the ins and outs of the loans were not important at that time. For me student loans boiled down to some paperwork I would complete a couple times a year and a $1,500 check I would receive at the start of each semester.

The loans were my new sustenance. Once formal college expenses were paid for (tuition, room, books, and meal plan), I lived on what was left over. Had I known what I know now about budgeting, saving, and investing, I would have gotten through each year fine on what I had left over from my loan. However, what I had witnessed in regard to finances was you spend as you have need, and, of course, a teenager's definition of need is not always need.

If I had known better, I would have sat down, looked at my school year, and written down the anticipated expenses for each semester. This is not too hard to do when you are a single young person in school. Each year's expenses are not going to vary too much. You know where you are going to be living (dorm or apartment), what you are going to be eating (cafeteria food), and what you're going to be spending extra money on (books and hanging out with friends). As I think back, it would have been so easy! My husband and I now have the planning process for our monthly budget down to a science where it takes about an hour to discuss the upcoming month. Oh, but to be single and in college! How simple it would have been.

Unfortunately, this big check I got at the beginning of each year would run out before the end of the year. Now, if you pick up any financial advice book, you will find that one of the biggest frustrations people have is not knowing where all their money is going each month. They know they receive a paycheck (or two) each month. They know that this paycheck theoretically should be covering all of their expenses (otherwise why would they have taken the job?). But at the end of the day they see the checking account is overdrawn, the savings account balance is zero, and the credit card balance is followed by three zeros. Where does all the money go?

I had no idea where my money was going because I did not make plans for it. Just as I gave the earlier

CHAPTER 2 THE COLLEGE YEARS

example of parents who make financial plans for their child to go to college, I should have been planning for where the loan money would go even before I received it. Think about someone expecting a baby. Do you wait until the baby arrives to get what you will need for it? No, you start to plan and prepare for the baby as soon as you find out that you are expecting. Why don't we have the same concept with money? Just as God entrusts us with children, He also entrusts us with money. We are responsible to Him to be good stewards of the money He entrusts us with. If we cannot be good stewards of the money we have, why would He give us more to waste? I was certainly not a good steward of my money in college and consequently I was always in need of more. It was not coming from anywhere that I could see, but one day I stumbled upon a new source of sustenance—credit cards!

The t-shirt made me do it. Sadly enough, I cannot even remember what the t-shirt looked like. But I knew I wanted it—no, I needed it! I walked up to the booth by the student union (very clever location) and asked the representative what I needed to do to get this t-shirt. "Just fill out this application for our 'fill-in-the-blank' credit card. If you're approved we'll send it out in 30 days. If not, the shirt is yours at no cost." No cost. Those two words will forever echo in my memory. There was a cost for that t-shirt, which I don't even have anymore, and it was not worth that cost! I filled out the application and took the t-shirt back to my dorm room for all my friends to see. I may even have persuaded some of them to sign up. (If any of you are reading this now, I apologize and please keep reading.)

In about a month's time I did get the card. If I remember correctly, I had a $1,000 credit limit and a $500 cash advance limit. I started off with just purchasing necessities like books and other school-related supplies on credit. However, later on I began using the cash advance option. I thought it was amazing. The first time I used it was a time when my rent was due. I had part of the rent, but not the entire amount. So I zipped to the ATM machine, popped in the card, and pulled out the cash. I clearly remember that moment—the ATM machine, the street I was on, and the relief I felt when the money came out. I was saved! Saved from what? The embarrassment of telling my roommates I did not have my share of the rent for one thing. But also, I now realized that I could get access to cash for social situations—when my friends and I made a last minute decision to go out for a bite to eat, for example. Even if my checking account reflected that I did not have any cash, I knew I had a source that I could go to in those situations of "need." Life was good.

With my credit card in hand I felt as though I was prepared for any financial pitfall that could possibly come my way. I mean, after all, I was paying the minimum payment of $15 every month so there would always be some money in my account, right? Yes, you read correctly—account. This is how I saw my credit card. In my eyes, the monthly minimum payment I was making was like depositing money into a savings account. So

Chapter 2 The College Years

my thought was that as long as I made deposits there would always be something left to take out.

Not!! Unbeknownst to me my balance was increasing every month; the nominal payments I was making were only keeping the phone calls from the creditors at bay. The credit card company was happy to accept my minimum payment because minimum payment means maximum interest for them. Cash advances had a different interest rate—even higher than using the credit card alone. And you already know about my cash advance dependency. Needless to say, after about six months the same money woes were at my doorstep again.

I am ashamed to say that the next path I took was begging. I did not see it as begging at the time; I thought of it as enjoying the benefits of a relationship. There were two men in my life at this particular time and I went to them both for money. I thought, "If they truly love me, they will do this." Today as a Christian, I know that this is called manipulation. But back then, as a fool, I took advantage of those closest to me. Did I get what I wanted from them? Sometimes I did and sometimes I didn't. Therefore I knew that this was not going to be a permanent solution to my money problems. There had to be a better way.

One of my parents talked to me about getting a job. Can you imagine?! It amazes me that all those years as a child I had worked for my father, yet I went away to college and thought that I was exempt from labor. Go figure. It certainly was not easy balancing books and burgers. (I worked at the fast food restaurants in the student union building.) But, I am writing to you as a college graduate so know that it can be done.

The money that I was making made a big difference, not only in providing for my expenses, but also in giving me a sense of responsibility. I was being awakened to the discipline aspect of money. In order to earn a paycheck, I needed to be disciplined enough to show up on time, learn what was expected of me, and then do it—all on my own. Working for my dad, I was obligated to be there. My parents shared in the responsibility of transporting me to work and making sure I did what needed to be done. There was no possibility (that I knew) of me getting fired. But with this being my first real job, I was responsible for keeping it. This made me value the money that I earned all the more because I was the only one accountable for earning it.

From this point forward, I was always working while I was in school, in addition to working during my summers off. The responsibilities grew as I went from preparing food to caring for people in nursing homes. But along with the responsibilities, I was growing, too. I could be depended on and was independent with my money. It felt good to finally have some control and to have some money left over at the end of the day.

CHAPTER 3

WORKING WOMAN

Personal Finances Personal Freedom

AFTER FIVE years of college, I had earned my Bachelor's of Science in Nursing. That unplanned fifth year, of course, added some extra debt onto my student loans, to which I was somewhat oblivious. I was doing better with money in that I had some. However, I still had my credit card debt and the student loan debt, which was about to be activated into full-fledged monthly bills.

I began working at the hospital where I had done my nursing clinicals during the last year of school. Receiving a five-figure salary was a real eye-opener for me. Never in my life had I thought about what it would be like to get paid like this—as well as receive benefits. There was a lot of paperwork and I filled it all out to get the job—not taking the time to find out what some of it meant to my financial future. Life was in the here and now. Certainly I wasn't thinking about retirement. Retirement?! I just got this job—I didn't want to retire. God protected me from several mistakes I could have made and let me make some other mistakes so that I would learn from them to be a better steward of His resources.

Young, single, and gainfully employed, I decided that I needed to make a purchase as proof of my independence. I had been eyeing several different vehicles for quite some time and had it narrowed down to three: a Chevy Cavalier, a Dodge Neon, or a Saturn. I ended up buying a brand new 1997 Chevy Cavalier

Chapter 3 Working Woman

at the first dealership I visited. I didn't check out the other two vehicles. I didn't even shop around for the best price on the Cavalier. And even more regrettably, I didn't bring anyone with me to help. I wanted to do this on my own. My feeling was that if I was responsible enough to get and keep a job, then I was responsible enough to get a vehicle by myself. I acted on emotions alone.

I remember the day I went to the dealership. It was a beautiful sunny day, perfect for buying a car. What's funny is I can remember the day, the salesman, and leaving with my new car; not much else. Obviously I had to have paid for the car, they wouldn't have let me just take it for free. But the financing business of it escapes my memory. I didn't have cash to pay, so certainly there was some kind of credit check involved. And for the next five years my car bill was sent from GM so I know that they were my creditors. However, I do not remember signing anything or discussing my loan in any specific terms. This was not of importance to me at the time.

What I do remember is the name of the car's color—Sandrift. Anyone who saw it would have said it was gold, but "Sandrift" sounded so elegant. The paint had sparkling flecks in it that glistened whenever the sunlight hit it. It was beautiful. Today I know that I could have probably bought a beautiful used gold Cavalier for half the price of the new one. But in my young mind, only new would do—new job, new car. Funny that the car-buying bug was catching. Almost every new graduate nurse that got hired around the time I did, bought a car—a brand new car. We all wanted what a new car represented—a spirit of independence. Never did I think about how my current independence would put a burden on my future marriage.

CHAPTER 4

The Two (Debts) Shall Become One (Big Debt)

HIS NAME was Ross and we were in love.

Actually his name is still Ross and, praise God, we are still in love! Ross and I met in college through mutual friends. Our relationship began in the best way, as a friendship. Eventually, however, we both began to see in the other, qualities that we desired in a mate. For me, I saw that Ross was gentle, considerate, and genuine. In me, Ross saw someone who was trustworthy and a good friend. Seeing these qualities in each other, drew us closer together and we began to date.

While we were dating, there were a few things that I noticed about Ross in regards to finances. He was a frugal man. I can say this was not the case when we would go out on dates. Whenever he would take me out to dinner, he would splurge and never set limitations on what I selected. But the grocery store was a whole different matter.

I can remember very clearly going grocery shopping with him one day during college. He knew the situation that I was in financially—how my money was not stretching through the semester. We were in the grocery store and I was looking for my favorite cereal "Honey Bunches of Oats." Well, Ross found on the shelf a generic version; let's call it "Golden Clusters of Flakes."

"Why don't you just get this one, Chanty? It's half the price of the one you want to buy and it's the same thing."

Chapter 4 The Two (Debts) Shall Become One (Big Debt)

"No, it's not the same thing. It has a different name."

"But, look. The ingredients are the same. It's the same cereal but they can sell it for cheaper because it's not a name brand. It will save you money."

"Ross, not everything is about saving money. Honey Bunches of Oats is the cereal I enjoy. I should be able to have the cereal I enjoy if I want it. It's not like it's that expensive."

The conversation probably went on a little longer, but I'm pretty positive I did not get the generic cereal. I got what I liked. I remember being raised this way. No, we didn't have a lot of money when my mom was raising us, but just the same we did not buy generic. No way! My mom got the name brand stuff for our food and household supplies. So naturally I continued to do what I knew.

Ross was raised by parents who were cautious in spending and lived within their means. I remember being amazed at how Ross had brought a deer heart to college to cook after hunting season one year. I was thinking, "Man, throw that thing away! That's the last thing I want to eat!" But he used it for soup. Another time we were having rotisserie chicken with some friends at school. We had eaten all of the bird, or so we thought. All of a sudden, Ross turns over the chicken and begins to eat the meat on the underside. "You all missed this!" I remember him saying with a big grin. He didn't waste much at all. His sense of frugality has been a major blessing to our marriage. But of course, I didn't see it that way in the beginning.

Personal Finances Personal Freedom

Ross and I had both accepted Jesus as our Lord and Savior during college. Upon graduating, we began attending a church together. Then, after considering marriage, we started taking pre-marital counseling classes. These classes discussed God's plans for marriage and also helped to bring about topics that we had never touched on previously.

The session that was the most memorable was the one on finances. The minister who met with us asked us at the previous class to write down our income as well as a list of our bills and other expenses, and then bring it to the next class. We were obedient to his request and brought in our information. After looking over what we had compiled he asked us, "Where do you want to live when you get married?" We told him we had planned to purchase a townhome. He very frankly told us that we did not have townhome money. Then after further inquiry, regarding our wedding plans, he added that we did not even have the money to pay for the type of wedding we were planning or the location where we were planning to have it. Between loans, credit card payments, and monthly bills, even with two professional incomes, our monthly income was pretty much equal to our monthly expenses. We were in no position whatsoever to even attempt to look at a townhome or have a big wedding in a big hall with all of our guests being served a formal dinner. (I need to mention here that Ross and I were paying for the wedding on our own.) The minister told us to re-vamp our budget and bring it back to him at the next session. His words stung like a slap in the face.

Chapter 4 The Two (Debts) Shall Become One (Big Debt)

After this class, Ross and I went for a long walk. We passed the hall where I had been planning to have my wedding. I remember stopping there and crying because, unlike that box of Honey Bunches of Oats, I couldn't have what I wanted this time. Inside I felt heartbroken, embarrassed, and angry. At first I was angry at the minister. After all we were fine with our plans until he meddled in them. But really I was angry with myself—angry with my irresponsible spending that led me to where I was now.

We sat that day and talked about a lot of things—options for where we could live affordably, how we could cut down on wedding expenses, and on and on. I certainly cannot say that it was easy. Never had I considered that money could ever be a hindrance to Ross and me becoming husband and wife. Sure, I could see lying, cheating, stealing—these were reasons to hold up an engagement or even cut it off. But debt? Everybody has debt. Married couples I knew had debt. What was the big deal? Well, I thank God for the wisdom of our pre-marital counseling minister. He wasn't looking at the here and now like I was. He saw past now into the future. Maybe he had even gone down the same road and was bent on turning others from going down that same dangerous path. Whatever the reason, God put him in our lives at that particular time and we are blessed for having had that encounter.

We went back to our next session the following week, me with my wounds in the process of healing and both of us with a lot more confidence than we had left with after the previous session! Sitting down with the minister we laid out our plan.

Originally we had wanted to buy a townhome but now we scrapped that idea. I was living at home with my mom so living in my current place of residence was out of the question. However, Ross was renting the bottom floor of a home with very affordable rent. We decided that we could live at his place to start out. It was an equal distance from both of our places of employment, so this plan was a winner.

The big hall on the river that I wanted to rent out for our reception wasn't gonna happen. So we looked into some other options. The church for the ceremony was already taken care of, and there was no fee for it. But we still needed a reception location. There was a newspaper article that we came across that listed local venues for having a wedding reception. One was a renovated barn in a nearby park. Guess the location? By the riverfront! Isn't God good? And so was the price. I think we rented it for under $100. Since there wasn't room for tables and chairs, we had chairs around the perimeter of the room only and had more of a "mingling" atmosphere. Even the food promoted mingling as it was "finger foods" that could be put on a plate and eaten with a toothpick or fork.

Speaking of the food, we made it all ourselves. At the time, my husband was the cook and I was usually the one who got the grunt jobs. By the time we were done, I was so sick of prepping the fixings to make quesadillas, crab cakes, and meatballs that I was ready to explode.

Chapter 4 The Two (Debts) Shall Become One (Big Debt)

I'm not sure where it is, but there is a picture that Ross took of me when I was about at my wit's end with the food preparation gig. You should see the look on my face—I didn't look like a bride about to be married. I looked like a woman scorned! Just the same, that prep work easily saved us hundreds of dollars in food expenses for our magical day. My husband was the ringleader in the idea of saving money by making our own food. He even orchestrated the "behind the scenes" stuff providing information on how it would be served, what it would be served on, and when it would be served. He is a true mastermind and I am so grateful to God for bringing him into my life.

In other areas, we trimmed in one of two ways—either scaling down on our original plans (i.e. going from a $600 gown to a $200 gown) or having services donated. My dad's new SUV became our limo. Skilled amateurs from our church videotaped and photographed the wedding. My hairstylist provided my hairdo as her wedding gift to me. All kinds of blessings began to occur once we made the decision to follow the counsel we had received and cut down our budget. This is a principle that still is at work in our lives today (more on that in chapter 9).

So this was our first glimpse at budgeting. But keep in mind that it was only a temporary process for us. We were not ready to buy (in) yet. We were just test-driving. Yes, it felt good to cut back and to not have to go into an excessive amount of debt on our wedding day. But we weren't planning to shape our lives around this concept. After all, we had a honeymoon to Aruba planned and the plan was to supplement (doesn't that sound like a non-threatening word?) paying for it with the credit card. We still were not ready.

CHAPTER 5

AFTER THE HONEYMOON

PERSONAL FINANCES PERSONAL FREEDOM

LIKE MOST couples, soon after the honeymoon had ended, life began to get stressful. Yes, there was the process of getting to know each other's habits and idiosyncrasies. There was also the fact that we had a honeymoon baby on the way! You think, "Chanty, that's enough to stress any new couple out!" Yes it was. But in addition to these factors was the money factor.

My definition of the term "money factor" is the underlying realization that finances affect and, in many cases, limit that which you desire for your lifestyle. I guess I should say that this was my definition. (My definition today is much different since I have learned how to properly treat money. I will share it with you at the end of the book.) It always seemed that lack of money had the upper hand. Yes, we could spend it when we didn't have it (using credit cards or getting loans). But money always had the last laugh because whatever we got was never worth what we paid, either due to interest accrued by the time we were able to pay it back, or simply because of depreciation—the value of what we got went down as soon as we got it! Again these are things I realize now, but didn't know then. At the time, I just summed my feelings up to being depressed over not having enough money. Sound familiar?

I blamed our money problems on my husband. It was his fault that I could not do certain things or buy

Chapter 5 After the Honeymoon

certain items. "If he wasn't so tight with the money I'd be able to enjoy being his wife a lot more," I would think. What I failed to realize was that Ross was justified in entering into a "conservative mode" in terms of our finances. Newly married and having a baby on the way, we couldn't afford not to save. But I viewed this as restrictive. It seemed everything we ate was made from "scratch" (no more frozen dinners or eating out). I was required to justify trips to see my family (leave and cleave—huh?), and clothes for my growing body were a luxury, not a necessity.

This was difficult for me to take. Now that we were married, scripturally I didn't have the option of accepting or declining his advice. No longer was it advice, it was leadership and he, as my husband, was my leader. But I resented his leadership. I longed for the days when I and I alone controlled how my money was spent—when if I wanted to splurge, I could. My mindset was not on how springing for a $5.00 lunch at McDonald's was going to affect our budget for the rest of the week. And why did I have to answer to him whenever I wanted to withdraw some money from the ATM? After all, it was our money, right? I can honestly say that I was in a single person's frame of mind—not wanting to answer to anyone for my money decisions.

Many arguments between Ross and I come to mind when I think about the beginning years of our marriage. And, admittedly, these arguments were a result of my selfishness. Selfishness in not considering others (my husband) before myself (Philippians 2:3,4). I was bent on feeding my desires in spite of the fact that I was defying my husband's leadership and putting our financial future in jeopardy.

On this note I must digress to clarify something. I was not single-handedly responsible for getting our family into the financial mess that we ended up in. My husband was in leadership over our family and he would tell you today that he made some decisions that contributed to the situation. However, I do take full responsibility for two specific areas where I failed in my role as a wife: 1) I was a manipulator and 2) I failed to be a revealer.

Webster's Dictionary defines the word manipulate as follows: "to control or play upon by artful, unfair, or insidious means especially to one's own advantage." Yeah, that was basically what I did. When it came to the subject of money, I would play my husband's heartstrings. It was either through whining and continually bringing up the subject of something I wanted to buy or through giving him the silent treatment—turning off affection when I did not get my way. Either way it is still manipulation and it is wrong. Instead of letting him lead me, I was causing him to loathe me.

Can you imagine? I was upset with him for leading in our relationship. Do you know how many women are dying for their man to lead in the marriage? I am in a women's discipleship group as I write this book and over half the women in my group have husbands who are not leading their families. The women handle the finances, make the decisions with the kids, take care of

Chapter 5 After the Honeymoon

the home, are sole attendees at church, and take out the trash.

By the way, taking out the trash is often how the whole role reversal thing begins in marriage. You ask your Honey to do it. He says, "Yeah, I'll do it, Baby." You look a moment later and it's still there. You look an hour later and it's still there. You look a day later and it's still there. What do you do? You take out the trash—after all the garbage man is coming tomorrow and if it doesn't go out, that trash will have to stay in your home another week. So what? You're telling me that instead of leaving trash in your home another week you'd rather deal with garbage in your home for the rest of your life?

The garbage I'm talking about is a bad marriage that stinks to high heaven because of all the responsibilities you've taken over that your man has been designed by God to handle. Take it from a woman who knows, **he will take out the trash.** All you need to do is have the patience to put up with the stink for a short while. Trust me when I say that the lifelong benefits will be well worth the wait.

I mentioned not being a revealer to my husband. Genesis 2:18 says, "The Lord God said, 'It is not good for the man to be alone. I will make a helper suitable for him'." You may feel as though you've heard this verse about a million times, especially if you are married. I used to think, "Yeah, yeah, yeah I know. I'm supposed to keep the home tidy and cook meals and do whatever other domestic stuff my husband doesn't have the skills to do. Got it." No, I didn't get it.

As Ross's wife, I am responsible for sharing with him the insight that God has given to me on specific issues. Whether it be insight I have from past experience, my career, or Scripture that I have read, as a helper I am responsible for contributing my share of wisdom to our marriage. When I fail to do this, I am in rebellion to who God has designed me to be. In this rebellion, our marriage suffered. Instead of revealing, I nagged—big difference.

When a wife reveals something to her husband, she picks the right time, the right setting, and the right attitude with which to share the issue. When a wife nags, she says whatever she needs to say whenever she feels like saying it and in front of whomever she wants to say it (unfortunately often times the "whomever" is the kids). Also a wife who is a revealer knows that she need only share with her husband one time. A wife who is a nagger feels that she cannot possibly be heard by sharing something just one time and proceeds to repeatedly "peck" at her husband. I was most definitely a nagging wife and therefore much of what I shared in the early years of our marriage was not received by my husband because I shared it in all the wrong ways.

Our shortcomings as a couple led us down a pretty rocky road financially. Starting out in marriage, we tried to do the right things. We always did work to balance the checkbook and keep a kind of loose monthly budget. The problem was that we did not stick to that budget. As things came up (or as I whined), we added onto whatever we had said we were going to spend each

Chapter 5 After the Honeymoon

month. Because of this inconsistency and other choices we had made as singles, we had a ton of debt. Both of us had credit card debt, a car payment, student loans, and a few personal loans. Now you may think, "That's normal for most Americans today." Well, I read something once that said because something is common, that does not make it normal. Say for example, in a certain town 80% of the population has cancer. Yes, it would be common in that town to have cancer, but, no, it is not normal to have cancer. In the same way, we as a society need to expose the myth that tens of thousands of dollars of debt is normal. **It is not!**

In spite of the debt, we worked hard at living "normal" lives. Normal to us at the time was trying to do and have most everything that those in our social circles had. This meant giving gifts with money we did not have to spend, buying a home without having a down payment, giving to fundraisers when we ourselves were in need of funds, and the biggest money-drainer—taking regular vacations on credit. For example, Ross and I were determined that we were going to go back to Aruba for our five-year anniversary. And by golly we did! However, airfare, lodging, and other expenses were all charged to 'old faithful'—the credit card. I remember how miserable it was seeing that vacation on our credit card statement month after month after miserable month! It was like the taste from a bad meal continuing to revisit you long after you've eaten it. Yuck! We knew that we'd done it to ourselves, but it still seemed unfair.

On another occasion, we had made plans to go out to eat dinner with some friends of ours. They picked the restaurant and we had heard of it but knew nothing about it. We arrived and it was an upscale, rather formal establishment. We were seated at the table and brought menus. I could only imagine what was going on inside my husband's mind as we sat staring at those menus. The prices were astronomical! We, being in debt up to our eyeballs, had absolutely NO business eating at this place. But we couldn't tell our friends that. It would be too embarrassing and they would know that we weren't like them. We didn't have money to spend like that. Then they might not want to be our friends anymore. That was what I thought at the time. We found out down the road that the wife of the couple was appalled by the prices as well and didn't think it was wise for them to have selected that particular restaurant. Like I said before, money got the upper hand again.

The Millionaire Next Door is an excellent book in which the authors Thomas J. Stanley and William D. Danko report the results of decades of research looking at how America's wealthy got that way. Interestingly enough, these individuals who we think of as going to the fanciest restaurants and driving the newest vehicles are surprisingly prudent in their behaviors. The book reveals that among other surprising lifestyle contradictions millionaires "... live well below [their] means. [They] wear inexpensive suits and drive American-made cars. Only a minority of [them] drive the current-model-year vehicle. Only a minority ever lease [their] motor

Chapter 5 After the Honeymoon

vehicles." (Thomas J. Stanley and William D. Danko, *The Millionaire Next Door,* Georgia: Longstreet Press. 1996, p. 9) This does not compute in our minds. We think more is more, when really less is more—that is, more money in our pockets. Status symbols like the latest model of BMW or the most recent version of iPhone are supposed to give the appearance of having money. In many cases, however, this is the furthest thing from the truth.

I can truthfully say that the money factor became the biggest contributor of discontent in our marriage. There were certainly other marital issues that we struggled with, but the issue of money was one that never seemed to get resolved. My husband would shut down when it came time to do anything related to finances.

Whenever we did come together to talk about our finances, we would both refer to it as "doing the bills" and I usually had to initiate. "Honey, when are we going to do the bills?" A groan would usually come from the other room. The way we referred to it was what it was to us at that time. All we did was pay bills. There was no savings or investing because there was nothing left to save or invest. It all went towards the bills. That's what it was and that's what we called it. Because we didn't enjoy this process (after all, what was there to enjoy?), our bills were often late which, in turn, generated late fees and dings on our credit report.

When I was single and out of college, I had been very diligent about paying my bills on time. Also, I thought that having a husband would give me the financial stability that I didn't have after my parents had divorced. Needless to say, I was not at peace and seriously doubted Ross's ability to take care of me and the now two children we had. These feelings showed up in my disrespect towards him and my unwillingness to submit to his leadership in many areas—not just financially.

With my husband not moving quickly enough to "do the bills," I jumped in to take over. (Remember the trash illustration?) Let me share with you that although I did the bills, I was not gifted in this area. Handling the details of finances is Ross's gift. However, being diligent about attending to the finances or any other matter is my gift. So it was decided that I would be the one to take care of paying the bills and balancing the checkbook. Unfortunately, I made some big mistakes in doing so.

The majority of those mistakes resulted in an overdrawn checking account and an irate husband. It seems I would routinely miss deducting ATM withdrawals from our balance and then have an over-inflated balance that truly was under-inflated. Ross would get so upset and I would just think in my head or say out loud, "At least our bills are getting paid. If it weren't for me everything would be overdue!"

If it weren't for me...I was putting myself in a position of sovereignty when only God can fill that position. If I would have just let the bills go, Ross would have stepped in. Yes, we may have taken some hits, but who would be responsible for those hits? Ross, the

Chapter 5 After the Honeymoon

husband. Instead, with me stepping out of position, who was now responsible for the hits? Me, the wife.

God is no fool. He knows what is best and He has it all planned out for us (Jeremiah 29:11). But His plan only works when we do what it says.

I mentioned my sin of manipulation in matters of money. A clear example of this was in me convincing, no, nagging my husband to get me a cell phone. At the time, we shared a cell phone that Ross carried with him most of the time. Well, after some time, I began to feel that I needed my own cell phone, too. I had seen many wives with their own cell phones and thought that this was just a given—a no-brainer. Did we live in the dark ages or what? Why were we sharing a cell phone? What if we were both traveling and needed to use it—then what?

Ross had taken over the budgeting by now and clearly saw that we should not be moving in the direction of taking on more bills. My justification was that my workplace had employee pricing that would give us a great deal. Plus we were personal friends with the cell phone representative which would put us in a position to get an even better deal. I protested, argued, and complained until Ross finally gave in. I'm sure it was out of sheer exhaustion rather than agreement.

Well, we got those wonderful new cell phones and guess what? First of all, I misunderstood some of the costs involved and we had to pay much more up front than what I had thought. The "deals" we were getting were through rebates that would not process and be refunded until several weeks later. However, we owed that money now and we did not have it in our budget to pay.

Second, I would regularly forget to carry or turn on the cell phone that I absolutely had to have. Consequently, Ross would call me and be fuming because why were we paying for a cell phone for me that I wasn't even operating?

Score another one for "the money factor."

Chapter 6

The Turning Point

In 2005, we became pregnant with our third child and began to discuss the need for a newer, bigger mode of transportation. Together we shopped around for a mini-van.

Although I have shared much about our money mishaps, there were also some times when we handled money wisely. Throughout our years of marriage we had received financial insight from various sources and would use these insights whenever we could. In this instance, we applied previous insight by looking at both new and used vehicles as well as shopping around for best prices and best quality. We also had learned about Consumer Reports ratings and the wisdom of looking at these ratings prior to making purchases. Going through this process of researching and waiting helped us to come to a decision together as to what van to buy. We felt that we had gone through steps the best we knew how in order to get the best deal possible. Initially we had to accept the dealer's financing to get a certain price. We later discovered that we could switch to our bank's financing which had a considerably lower interest rate. We did the best that we knew how with this purchase and this was a victory for us.

In February 2006, we had a new little one which brought us to a total of three children—in case you lost count. It had been some time since our last major

Chapter 6 The Turning Point

financial catastrophe. The previous summer our family had taken a trip to Disney World that was partially financed by credit and partially paid for in cash so I felt like we were moving in the right direction—not completely there but getting better, right?

I had mentioned previously that we now owned a home. Although it was only 12 years old, various appliances became in need of being replaced. This is one of those givens of being a homeowner. But needless to say, it caught us off-guard and unprepared every single time. Not that you can plan when something is going to break down, but financially it just never seemed to happen at a good time. We would get an income tax refund and have big plans of paying something off when all of a sudden the hot water heater went out. Or we just emptied the checking account to pay bills and next thing you know the dryer went kaput! There's an old saying that says to expect the unexpected. We couldn't have lived further from this teaching. Our financial survival revolved around a delicate balance of stable incomes, consistent debt, and certainly no surprises!

It was nerve-wracking, to say the least, when each surprise would rear its ugly head. I remember thinking, "Okay this house is only going to get older and older. Eventually every single appliance will need to be replaced and we do not have the means to do that." Again wanting to keep up with "the Joneses" (having the home like other families we knew), got us in over our heads. We hadn't planned; we just drooled—drooled over the prospect of having what everyone else had. We just wanted in, not considering the cost.

For the past year or so, we had been having some problems with the heat pump in our home. These problems were most notable in the summertime when the heat would get to the point of being unbearable. We would often retreat to the basement to escape the sweltering temperatures in the house. It even felt cooler outside at times than it did in our home. We had the Freon in the pump replaced on a couple of occasions and that ran us over $300 each time! Well, finally when we had the pump looked at in the summer of 2006 the specialist told us that it needed to be replaced. The Freon that had recently been added was already gone. Can you imagine?! Three hundred dollars down the drain just like that. How disgusting!

So we needed a new heat pump. That was all fine and good. The fact of the matter though is that heat pumps run between $7,000 and $10,000. We didn't have that kind of money. So what did we do? We waited.

That summer in our house was agonizing. My husband and I had the luxury of having a ceiling fan in our room. For us the fan combined with opening the windows and sleeping with no sheets gave us some relief. Our children's rooms were another story. I can remember putting portable fans as a line item in our August 2006 budget. Things were already tight that month (as with every month) but this was a necessity.

Chapter 6 The Turning Point

We were only able to purchase two so we got a stationary fan for our daughter's room to blow air directly onto her and a rotating one for the boys' room that would blow air from one to the other. It helped, but the heat was still overwhelming.

One evening after the kids had been tucked into bed, my husband and I went to check in on them in their rooms before retiring for the night ourselves. Upon doing so we saw something that ripped our hearts in two. Our baby boy lay in his crib, sleeping soundly, his hair pasted to his head from the sweat dripping out of him. Around his head on his sheets was a wet outline—like one of those crime scene outlines the police make when someone is murdered. I felt like the criminal that night—a criminal for robbing my children of the comfort that is supposed to be part of a home. Right there and then I was slapped in the face with the reality of the devastation that my poor decisions had made. That moment we both knew that it was time for a change—and we were finally ready.

Personal Finances Personal Freedom

Chapter 7

Reading, Writing, and Arithmetic

WHERE TO begin? We had a big mess on our hands and no idea whatsoever how to start cleaning it up. We're talking years of bad habits, bad decisions, and bad credit. It already seemed like hard work doing what we were doing—making ends meet each month. I couldn't even begin to imagine the work involved in managing our money the right way. What I didn't realize was that managing our money was hard because we weren't ever truly managing it.

During the fall of 2006 Ross and I went back to school. We began our own personal classes in "Financial Freedom." It began with us being in agreement with the fact that the way we were currently handling our money was not responsible, not purposeful, and not working! Once we could agree that we were both at fault (We weren't just in this mess because of me spending too much on the kids or Ross picking up late night caffeine.), then it was easier to begin the process of repairing the damage.

My husband and I both love to read but, like many people, have difficulty in making the time to do so. Ross came up with the plan of checking out books on finances from the library. He would check out so many at a time and then divide them up for us both to read. He later shared in a testimony that his personal goal was to read the majority of the books since he was the head of our family and wanted to take on the largest

Chapter 7 Reading, Writing, and Arithmetic

portion of responsibility in getting us out of debt. What a gentleman!

Having the common goal of financial freedom did something wonderful for our marriage. We experienced a unity and a peace that we hadn't shared before this time. I felt like we were both on the same side—no longer were there the same sources of conflict over money. We had decided upon what we wanted to do together. If what we wanted to do individually didn't fit what we had decided upon together, it was out of the question. For example, I may have wanted to buy that bag of chips in the convenience store on the way home from work. However, buying that bag of chips moved us further away from the goals we had set, so I had to practice restraint. Do you see what I'm saying? Once the two of us had put managing our finances on the radar as a priority in our family, the temptation to spend selfishly or impulsively fizzled out. There is even Scripture to support this fact. Amos 3:3 says, Do two walk together unless they have agreed to do so? Ross and I were in agreement to walk together and it made the road we were on that much smoother.

As we read, we wrote. We took notes to share with each other on what each book was about, what we learned from it, and what we could apply to our own family. Every two weeks, we would have an official meeting to discuss our findings. I looked forward to those meetings—I even miss them now. It was so exciting to get information about what we could do better. I understand now why it is said that knowledge is power. How true this is! With the information we obtained from the books, I felt empowered. I always thought that the money we had coming in was our only resource. Ah, but there is so much more! I look forward to sharing with you many of the methods that we have learned to use our money wisely.

We continued on with our meetings through January 2007. We had read dozens of books between the two of us by then. Even though we weren't having our official meetings, we continued to read books and even listened to books on tape while we were in our vehicles. God had placed a passion and an excitement for financial freedom inside of us. I can remember talking, dreaming, and planning towards the day that we would not be strapped with debt. Finally that day seemed like it was in our grasp—not something that we had to wait for, but something that was not far down the road. It was an exciting time!

Chapter 8

Putting it into Practice

I TALKED in Chapter 5 about already having a budget of sorts in place. However, just because someone has a budget, it doesn't mean that they are living by it. That was us.

Each month we entered numbers into a spreadsheet with our expenses and our income. And practically every month our income fell short of our expenses. Well, the reason for this was simple—we were not sticking to the budget. Every month we would allow the "lust of the eye" to tempt us (1 John 2:16). The Bible says that this lusting comes from the world, not from God. We allowed what we saw here on earth to dictate how we would spend God's money. Yes, God's money. It is key to understand that your money is provided by and belongs to the Lord. You may say, "But I give God His 10% every paycheck. I thought the rest was mine to keep." Wrong. Physically we do have possession of the 90% or whatever the case may be. But we are stewards of that money and should be open to doing with it what God tells us to do. My husband and I have been committed to passing this truth along to our children.

Since they were babies at Christmastime we make a point of telling them that Santa does not bring their gifts. Instead we share with them that God has provided Mommy and Daddy with jobs that pay us money to be able to buy them presents, food, and anything else we get. The Bible says to train up a child in the way that

Chapter 8 Putting It Into Practice

they should go so that when they are old they do not depart from it (Proverbs 22:6). I will share with you in Chapter 10 other ways in which we have trained our children in understanding the truths about money.

So before putting a budget down onto paper, we looked at what we were spending money on in the past few months. When I talked to my husband before writing this chapter, he used the analogy of a sinking boat to describe our tactic. If a boat is sinking, what is the first thing that you do? Stop the leaks. Once you stop the leaks, the problem that is causing you to sink (water) is remedied. Then you can proceed with bailing out the water so that you can float again. In terms of our budget, the leaks were a result of frivolous spending.

Whether our spending was frivolous or not was best determined by thinking in terms of needs versus wants. We looked at expenses such as contributions towards school fundraisers for our own kids as well as our friends' kids and often made the decision not to support them. When we were invited to parties where gifts were expected, we carefully considered our relationship with the person as opposed to readily accepting the invitation simply because we received it. Ross and I even made decisions together on certain occasions as to whether or not I would go visit my mother who lived about 15 minutes away. (While we were going through this process of watching our spending, gas prices were sky high!) No, these weren't easy decisions or popular decisions. They were difficult decisions that sometimes felt downright stifling. We kept in mind, however, that these decisions were only for a time. During this season, they moved us closer to our goal and ultimately closer to God. We had begun to take the time to consider what the best use of God's money was and this pleased Him. I could just see Him smiling!

Although a need seems fairly straightforward, this isn't always the case. One person may be willing to wear a pair of shoes and decide that not until they fall apart around their foot is it time for another pair. Another person buys a new pair every six months because of the physical wear that they put on the shoes. In this same way between my husband and I, there was a significant difference in the evaluation of the needs of our kids where clothes were concerned.

When it would come time to "do the bills" I would timidly bring up the need for underwear, socks, shoes, or clothes of any kind for the kids. I remember bringing up the need for "casual shoes" for our daughter on one occasion. Ross could not wrap his mind around the fact that our daughter needed casual shoes. "She has a pair of dress shoes and a pair of sneakers. Her sneakers are her casual shoes!" he barked. Now to his credit my husband has softened a lot since then and if I mention a need for the children he puts it into the budget with little argument. But this is because he can trust me now. I used to manipulate, complaining that the kids would need this and that. He would realize that what I had asked for wasn't a true need and would get angry about it—rightfully so. It took some time for him to begin to trust me in spite of my track record. Building

Chapter 8 Putting It Into Practice

back this trust included taking him to the kids' closets to see what clothes they had, examining shoes for wear and tear, etc. That was humbling for me but it was necessary. It was also part of the process that helped us learn to bring all of our information to the table and talk out any differences in opinion so that we could reach an agreement together.

As I shared, we had already had a budget but we began to commit to living by it. The kind of budget that we work from is called a "zero balance budget." Using this kind of budget, all of your income is allocated (assigned) to an expense until you have zero dollars left. Now when I first read about this type of budget I thought it sounded plain stupid. Why would I want to plan to spend all of my money? Wasn't that what got us into all this trouble in the first place? No, what got us into all of the trouble we were in is that we were spending without planning. With a zero balance budget if all of your money is pre-assigned, there is no room for impulse spending. You spend what you have. Even if you see a great pair of size 12 shoes on sale and you can never find shoes in your size and you really need a new pair of black heels and they fit you just right and would go perfect with that dress for your sister Sally's wedding and on and on and on—you cannot buy them. It's that simple.

Now you say, "Chanty what if a need comes up, not a want, but a need for the month and I forgot to calculate it into my monthly budget?" Well, that's simple. You take the money for your need from another assigned expense. For example, you have planned in your budget one take-out pizza night for your family. In the middle of the month you get sick and need to purchase a prescription for an antibiotic. You take the money that you would normally have used to get the pizza and get your medicine instead.

Now you may still have some money left for eating out, so you have three options.

1. You may decide to eat out and have the family order off of the dollar menu.
2. You could still have pizza, but buy it frozen from the grocery store, or buy ingredients to make your own. (We do this all the time.)
3. You could just skip eating out for the month.

When you're trying to get out of debt, the initial stages are not always fun or comfortable for everyone. But keep in mind, they are just initial stages. These beginning steps are what will start to eat away at your debt little by little and, more importantly, build a foundation of how to make decisions about money for a lifetime.

I won't tell you how to make your budget. There are so many options and all kinds of software programs in existence now that the possibilities are endless. I will tell you that we don't use any software, so please know that you don't have to spend any money to come up with a good budget. My husband has our monthly

Chapter 8 Putting It Into Practice

budgets on Excel spreadsheets. He is a genius when it comes to spreadsheets. I can navigate them pretty well but he puts formulas into them and all kinds of other functions that I would have to follow a guide to understand. At the time of this writing, our budget basically consists of three columns (as many columns as there are paychecks that we receive for the month). Underneath our paycheck amounts at the top are our expenses beginning with tithes and offerings, on down to bills, etc.

Before the beginning of each month, Ross and I meet for about an hour to talk about our finances. We begin by praying together, and then we look over a skeleton budget. This is the "template" budget that includes all of the expenses that are in a given month—things like the electric bill, gasoline, mortgage payment—things that we all know are expected to be paid each month. It's easy to plan for these items. During this meeting we look at our calendar and then add in any additional expenses that do not occur on a monthly basis. These include a doctor's visit co-pay, a gift for a baby shower, a new shower curtain, etc. By doing this we are able to think of the majority of expenses for each month. We have almost always missed something pretty much every month. But, today we are at the point where we can add it into the budget without taking from other areas. (Praise God!) But in the beginning, we looked to see: 1) if it was a need or a want, and 2) if it was a need, where we would take the money from to pay for it.

Once we began to stick to our budget, we moved to the next step of saving money. This was also a part of the process of stopping the leaks in the sinking boat. A few of the books we read, emphasized having a savings account with $1,000 in it before beginning to pay off debt. Again, I have to say I was skeptical thinking, "We are in debt and we are in debt because we don't have money to pay off the debt. Where are we supposed to find money to put aside $1,000 in savings? We've never had $1,000 in the bank before without it being slated to pay for something."

Well, to this day I don't know where that $1,000 came from, but we did it! I shared with you in Chapter 4 that as we began to make wise decisions with our money, God began to give us more of it. Whether it was $5 here or $100 there, whatever came in we readily saved. It was exciting to save especially knowing that we had a short-term and a long-term goal. The short-term goal was to save $1,000 and the long-term goal was to get out of debt. In two months, we had $1,000 saved in a money market account. Two months! The time went really quickly because we were so focused and God provided so readily.

The reason for saving $1,000 is to have money to pay for unexpected expenses. I'm not talking about the pizza versus the antibiotic illustration. I'm talking about the car that breaks down or the hot water heater that goes kaput. Those emergency expenses that every household has are the ones that can put you right back into debt again (or further into debt in the beginning stages). Like us, in many circumstances when there

CHAPTER 8 PUTTING IT INTO PRACTICE

is no money, you pull out the plastic and dig a deeper hole. When you do this, it negates all of the progress you've made up until that point. However, if you have an emergency savings account, you can pay cash for those mishaps without going back to the plastic.

The important thing to remember is that when you spend money from this account, you need to work to replace it right away. **The emergency savings account needs to always remain at a $1,000 balance so that you no longer need to rely on credit.** This means that even once you've started paying off debt, if you have an emergency and need to take money from the account, stop paying on your debt until the account is back at $1,000. Consider the deficit you've made in your savings account your debt to pay off in the time being.

Something important to remember is that this savings account is for emergencies only. Hopefully everyone who has read this far is clear on what a need is and what a want is. Another thing I want you to be clear on is what an "emergency" is. No one puts it more plainly than financial guru Dave Ramsey. He says this in his book, *The Total Money Makeover*.

> Most of America uses credit cards to catch all of life's "emergencies." Some of these so-called emergencies are events like Christmas. Christmas is not an emergency; it doesn't sneak up on you. Christmas is always in December, they don't move it, and therefore it is not an emergency. Your car will need repairs, and your kids will outgrow their clothes. These are

73

not emergencies; they are items that belong in your budget. If you don't budget for them, they will feel like emergencies. Americans use the credit cards to cover actual emergencies too. Things discussed earlier, like job layoffs, are real emergencies and are the reason for an emergency fund. A leather couch on sale is not an emergency. (Dave Ramsey, *The Total Money Makeover: A Proven Plan for Financial Fitness*, Thomas Nelson, Inc., 2009, p. 104)

There is a saying I believe most people have heard that says, "Poor planning on your part does not constitute an emergency on my part." Do not use your emergency savings account to cover expenses caused by your lack of responsibility. I say this not as a put down but as a hand up. You are only hurting yourself and your financial future when you refuse to use money in the proper way. I am writing this book because my desire is to help others to get out of what God has freed me from. So if you have this book consider me your coach; trust me and do as I say. ☺

CHAPTER 9

DEBT DEMOLITION

FINALLY! WE were living by a budget and had saved $1,000 for emergencies. Hallelujah! Our next step was to pay off our debts. Our debts at this time included:

    $8,100 for a home equity loan

    $3,200 in student loans for me

    $3,400 in student loans for Ross

    $2,300 car loan

    $21,000 van loan

    $6,100 credit card bill

That's a total of **$44,100 in debt.** Just seeing that number on paper I am amazed all over again at what God has done. At the time it certainly seemed like the impossible dream. But today it is a testimony to what God is able to do.

Books and other sources that we looked to suggested several different theories as to which debt to tackle first. We liked and followed the suggestion of paying off debts starting with the smallest balance and ending with the largest balance, regardless of what the interest rate was. It will take a shorter amount of time to pay off the smaller debts, and believe me, you will appreciate the motivation of seeing the fruit of your labor sooner rather than later. When you start with paying a debt that you can pay off in say two to three months, it gives you more immediate results that will help you to stay the

Chapter 9 Debt Demolition

course. If we were to take on our $21,000 van loan as our first debt to pay off, I don't believe that it would have resulted in the same momentum that we experienced by paying off our car in five months, then my student loan three months after that, etc. Let's face it, we are human and we thrive on rewards for our achievements. Pursuing your debts in this way will help motivate you to finish strong.

To begin paying off our debt, we needed to find "extra" or "hidden" money to put toward it. Some of the books that we read gave suggestions as to how to do this. A big piece in getting extra money was really just in better handling the money that we already had coming in. Neither one of us had to get another job or work anymore overtime than we normally did. We simply made changes to the way we spent money and eliminated some of the unnecessary things that our money was going towards. I'll give you a few examples.

Food is a **BIG** area of expense for most families and actually one of the easiest ways to find extra money to put towards debt. A book that I read, talked about using menu planning as a strategy to save money. It is difficult to go into a grocery store without cringing at the prices that food is going for these days! One can easily spend $200 there and not have it last for two weeks—no matter what size family you have. The book suggested making a menu of what meals you will have during each week. Just like we talked about with the zero balance budget, when you have a plan, it is easier to stick with the plan. Without a plan, you do whatever seems best. When you're in the grocery store, buying a meat package, the most recently advertised cereal, and a gourmet dessert may seem best. But if you don't have a plan for those items, they will spoil or be eaten up in two days! We began to make menus before going grocery shopping. The menus were based on what foods we already had and what foods we could purchase inexpensively. This way we were not letting anything go to waste and we were not paying a lot of money for our meals.

Other simple ways you may or may not have already thought of to cut back on food expenses include:

- Eating out less
- Packing lunches for work and school
- Controlling portion sizes and "bottom-less seconds"
- Taking coffee from home instead of buying it at coffee shops
- Eating leftovers or saving them for potluck at the end of the week

We have a family of five (our children are currently four, eight, and nine) and when we began the process of getting out of debt, we set a spending allowance of only $100 every two weeks for groceries. Yep, you read it right! Sticking to a menu helped us to do this. We also shopped at specific stores to get the best prices. In the area where we live there are several discount grocery stores that we take full advantage of. On average we go

Chapter 9 Debt Demolition

to three different stores every two weeks to shop for our groceries. Some people don't like to do this because they say that it wastes time and gas. Well, we don't zip from one place and then across town to another. Instead we cluster our shopping with other errands we need to run in that same vicinity. This way we are not going out of our way just to get groceries at a great price.

Today our grocery budget has increased to $140 every two weeks. This is still a lot less than most people spend. We made the change because groceries cost more now than they did four years ago and our children have grown and now have higher caloric needs for their bodies. I completely avoided saying "our children have bigger appetites" in order to make my next point. Adults need to set limits on eating for their children. I'm not even going to go into the obesity epidemic because we are all aware of it. What I will say is that today it is no big deal for a child to devour two or three adult-sized servings of food and no one blinks an eye at it. Every meal has become "supper-like," being comprised of lots of food with lots of calories. Think about buffets—you pick the meal (breakfast, lunch, or dinner) there's a buffet for it! We are inadvertently teaching our kids that it is okay to eat a lot instead of putting the emphasis on eating well. Believe me, I am guilty of this at times as well. But I have always been aware of it.

One of the things that we did with our children is that when they packed their school lunches, we had a list of options posted on the fridge. With those options, there were also limits. For example, if one of the options was baby carrots, there was written next to it the number "5" which meant that they could take up to five baby carrots in their lunch. Not only did this help us with controlling how much money we spent on food, but it also helped us to make sure that they were not eating more than they needed. I've heard stories from friends of how their children (tots and teens) are bottomless pits when it comes to food to the point where they buy groceries multiple times a week to keep food in the house. In many instances this can be avoided if parents provided appropriate servings. Just as I shared earlier about needs versus wants in the realm of finances, the same can be taught to children as it relates to food.

Switching our credit card debt to another credit card with a lower interest rate was another way that we chose to decrease our monthly expenses. This is called a balance transfer. Now, I must throw in a disclaimer here. Some credit card companies will give you a low interest rate on transferred balances, but it is only for a period of time. After so many months they will jack the interest rate up and with good reason—they now can earn a sky high interest on the debt from all those cards you transferred over! So make sure to read the fine print. By doing some online research, Ross came across a special version of a name brand credit card. When we looked into it, we found that the interest rate was only 4.99% compared to the hefty double-digit interest rates that our current credit cards were carrying. We transferred all of our card balances to this lower interest rate card, and then diligently made our minimum

Chapter 9 Debt Demolition

monthly payments until it was time to stack all of our money onto this debt (more on that coming up).

Quite a while back when we were just dabbling in learning about managing our money more wisely, a friend from church had shared with us about a method she and her husband used called the envelope system. Whenever they had a budget expense that required cash, they would take the necessary amount of cash out of the bank and put it into an envelope labeled with the name of that particular expense. When it came time to pay for that expense, they would take the labeled envelope with them, and pay with the money in the envelope instead of writing a check or using a debit card.

You may wonder what the reasoning is for this. It's all about discipline. Having cash on hand significantly decreases the chances of overspending in a particular area. When you have decided on an amount, taken the time to go to the bank and withdraw the money, and have it in an envelope with you, a sense of obligation kicks in. You didn't go through all that trouble just to pull out your debit card and blow your budget. Instead you work to do the most you can with the money that you have on hand. For myself, having cash on hand helps me to prioritize and to scale down when my tendency would be to splurge.

Examples of some expenses where you may use the envelope system are:

- Eating out
- Shopping for clothes
- Buying groceries

- Purchasing a gift
- Vacation expenses
  (meals, souvenirs, etc.)

All of these expenses are ones which: 1) have no definite allowance, and 2) may tempt you to spend more money than you had originally planned. Having the money in that envelope, serves as a visual reminder that you have set a boundary on your spending and it serves as motivation to keep that boundary in place.

My stylist smiles every time I take out my envelope to pay her after my hair appointments. I love my envelopes! They are battered and have a lot of writing crossed out on them as we have reused them for many different expense categories. We don't get rid of them until they have holes in them from the weight of the coins they have held over a period of months.

That raises a good question—what do you do if you have money left over in your envelopes? Say you went to shop for clothes and you did such a good job bargain hunting that you still have $10 left in your clothes budget. What do you do with the extra $10? Well, if you are still in the process of eliminating debt that $10 goes toward whatever debt you are currently working to pay off. If you are out of debt, you can keep that money in the shopping envelope and use it when there is another clothing item you may need or if another expense comes up during the month (which it inevitably will), you can use it to go toward that expense. Of course, it does not hurt to save that $10 either. It all adds up!

Chapter 9 Debt Demolition

You might feel that carrying around cash is a temptation. I cannot remember one time during that season of saving when I was tempted to spend my "envelope money" on something that it wasn't meant for. What I can remember is being in awe of people who would have cash on hand—just hanging out in their pockets! This never fazed me before. In fact, my dad has always been this way. He just always has cash on him. But for us, because we were dead focused on deleting our debt, every penny was accounted for in the budget. There was no cash to "hang out." If we had extra, we were putting it somewhere—and it was usually towards debt.

A simple habit that will save cash is paying your bills on time. It is amazing what the late fees are for bills and credit cards. I can remember one credit card that we were consistently late in paying would result in an additional $35 charge every month. Remember, that this $35 is then tacked onto the original balance and gets charged interest right along with it. $35 may be the amount of your water bill or your gym membership. Either way, it is money that is unnecessarily going to waste each month.

If you have the money to pay your bills, and just aren't very organized to get them paid on time, I suggest that you do one of two things. One tactic is to use folders for organizing your bills. A friend of mine keeps hers on the kitchen counter where she'll be sure not to miss them. When you get the bills for the month, group them by "to be mailed by" dates. Therefore, bills with similar due dates will be mailed out together so that they will reach their destination before the due date.

Another tactic is to pay your bills online. I don't know of any banks that do not have online banking these days. It has been a blessing to us because late fees were one of our problems. Online banking allows you to set up ahead of time what date that you would like your account to be credited for a bill. You can set a monthly date for each bill to be paid, or you can pay your bills on a day by day basis.

Either way, online banking offers convenience and helps in developing the discipline that sometimes is lacking in managing personal finances. Because of computer security issues, some people prefer not to bank online, and I can completely understand. You'll have to choose a method with which you are most comfortable. Even if you choose another method of getting organized, it will be worth it to get back this 'free' money every month.

These are just a few examples of ways to find money within your budget. Now some people may take on extra work or overtime in order to have more money to put toward their debt. Sometimes this is the answer, but not always. I recommend asking God what He wants you to do. As I shared, my husband and I never had to take on additional work at our jobs in order to pay off debt. The work that we did take on was homework—setting up a workable budget, educating ourselves on money management, and committing to stick to a financial plan. I believe that the process we went through was just as

Chapter 9 Debt Demolition

tough as working a second job or overtime. But it paid off and we are now on the other side of the victory. I am praying that you will be, too.

Once we found the extra money, we started by paying on our car loan. If you remember, this was our lowest debt. We were already making the monthly payment, which was about $400. Now our commitment was to pay $400 plus whatever extra money we could add to it each month. Sometimes it would be $100 and sometimes it would be $200. Whatever the amount, we knew that we were making strides towards getting closer to having that particular debt paid off.

My husband created two graphs of our debts: one that projected when we would have each one paid off and one with the actual date that the debts were paid off. To look at the two graphs, one could easily see God's hand at work. In all instances, our debts were paid off anywhere from a few months to a few years prior to when we thought they would be.

I continue to encourage you that when you are doing what is right with what God has given you, He will step in and do supernatural things for you. This is what He did in our finances and to this day I stand in awe of how He has blessed us! We began paying down our car debt in January and had paid off the car completely by June. Having that one victory under our belt felt great and we did celebrate. It is important to celebrate your victories even while living on a budget. This is an exciting time and certainly one that you want to stop and rejoice over as you reach your short-term goals along the way.

While you are putting extra money toward a particular debt, it is important to note that **you are only making the minimum payments on any other debts that you have.** Do not put any extra money toward them at this time. During this time you will pour all of the extra money you can get your hands on into the lowest debt. Concentrating your efforts on one source will help you to reach your goal more quickly and serves as the motivation you will need to continue doing what you're doing. Each debt will have its time to be paid down in the order we spoke of earlier.

So we paid off our car, and we were on to our next debt, my $3,200 student loan. Let's say the monthly payment for that was $200. Now we are paying $200 towards this loan plus any extra money that comes in during each month.

But wait—guess what's "extra money" now—that $400 that was going towards our car loan. Remember we had budgeted $400 towards a car payment every month. Well, the car payment is no longer, but the money is! So now we had $600 plus going to my student loan every month. Do you see the beauty in all this? As you pay off each debt, the amount you are able to put towards the remaining debt grows and the time it takes to pay off each remaining debt shrinks because you are putting more money toward it than you ever had to put toward it before! As I write I'm jumping for joy because I LOVE this concept! I've heard it called a "debt snowball" or "stacking payments." I call it glorious! We started paying on my student loan in June and had finished

Chapter 9 Debt Demolition

paying it off in September. Ross's student loan was paid off the following month. How cool is that!

I can certainly remember the excitement of paying off our car and being amazed that we had paid it off early. But equally exciting was seeing the subsequent debts diminish before our eyes. It amazed me how quickly each one decreased once we paid off that initial car debt. Each month I would wait with bated breath to see how much we were able to pay down on the next debt in line and how much closer that would bring us to paying off all of the debt. The closer we came to paying off something, the easier it was to "buckle down" in our spending. Yes, I wanted that dress but I also wanted my American Express card paid off. Yes, my husband wanted to eat out with his co-workers, but he wanted to pay off our home equity loan more. Seeing the reality of debts dwindling down before our very eyes made denying ourselves a piece of cake.

Dave Ramsey has a mantra that states "If you will live like no one else, later you can live like no one else." In other words, do the "hard" things now (not eating out, cutting back on recreation, packing lunch, doing your own nails, working overtime) so that one day you will be able to live a life where you can dictate where your money goes instead of your debt having the final say. We had our eyes on the prize of a bigger goal which would have far greater satisfaction than any temporary piece of clothing or morsel of food could ever give.

As we sat down to do the bills—I mean plan our finances for the month, it was thrilling to me to see what

God was doing. To think that He took me from a place of not believing that we could ever be out of debt to seeing the debt decrease month after month, was a true miracle! Certainly not a reality that I thought I'd ever see. Most of my adult life my mindset had been when the money comes in, you spend as you have need—and sometimes you even spend before the money comes in! Planning where to put my money each month (aside from bills) was not a part of my make-up. So how a woman with this make-up can move from one extreme to the other is surely an act of only our Lord and Savior.

We continued on the course of pouring as much money as we could into the next debts in line. It reminded me of one of those video games, from my younger days, where you shoot and shoot at the opponent until he is obliterated into little cubes that scatter on the screen. With each debt, we fought to "hit" it with as much money as we could each month until it was obliterated and we could mark "paid" next to it on our graph. It was thrilling for me to watch the debts evaporate before my very eyes. Although I knew that putting money towards debt would pay it down, I still was in amazement each time a debt got paid off. Never in my life could I remember a time when I'd purposed to pay off rather than create debt.

Our credit card was the next debt in line after our student loans. I shared with you that plastic was how we dined, vacationed, shopped, and took care of unexpected expenses. Payments were always a drag because we were paying off the past—something that had come and gone but the monthly memory lived on.

Chapter 9 Debt Demolition

When we paid off the credit card, I was elated. I felt like not only had we paid off the past, but we had also put a bad habit behind us. To us, the credit card was a symbol of slavery that we no longer wanted to bear. Hallelujah to be free of that burden!

We do still use credit on occasion. Some instances are: paying for reimbursable work-related expenses and paying for online purchases. Also, we may use a store credit card to get a percentage discount on a purchase. However, we make sure that we have the money to pay for that purchase even though we are putting it on credit. There have been times when we have even paid the credit card off before leaving the store!

Our next to last debt was the home equity loan for the heat pump. Having to take out a loan to pay for this appliance was not something that we were happy about. However, the wake-up call that God gave us as a result of taking out the loan to pay for the heat pump is an experience we would not trade for the world. He knew what needed to happen to shake up our world. Our wake-up call to change our money management was our children's discomfort. What is yours? Is it illness? Loss of a vehicle? Loss of a job? Death of a loved one? Or is it just being sick and tired of having your money already spent before you even receive your paycheck? Whatever the case may be, God can provide you with victory over your finances. You don't have to continue to live the way that you're living just because it's the way you've always lived.

I know I'm speaking to someone. This is how I felt. "Why change now? I've done this dance for years. Yes, I get tired of not having enough money, but I still live a blessed life." Understand that God wants the very best for you. His Word says that Jesus came that we may have life and have it to the full (John 10:10b). He doesn't want us to have an okay life. He wants us to have a fulfilled life—one that doesn't miss one ounce of what He intends for us to share in. Ordering our finances is part of His blessing. There is such peace when He holds the reigns to the money that He has provided us stewardship over.

When we paid off our heat pump, it was like everything had come full circle. Yes, we had to learn our lesson the hard way. (Remember that no discipline is pleasant at the time, but painful.) However, it brought us to the point of doing things God's way so that we could experience the path to being healed of our financial troubles. (Later on, that discipline reaps a harvest of righteousness and peace for those who have been trained by it.)

December 26, 2008, is the date my husband and I became consumer debt-free after nine years of marriage. We paid off our van online while visiting my in-laws over the Christmas holiday. I remember us gathering them along with the kids into the computer room to share with them what we were about to do. Although everyone respectfully gathered to commemorate the occasion, only Ross and I truly had an understanding for what this payment meant.

Chapter 9 Debt Demolition

A little less than two years earlier we had a TWENTY-ONE THOUSAND DOLLAR van loan. I had to write that in caps because you may have misread the figures I listed earlier in the chapter. And now even after writing it down, it still seems like it can't be possible. We purchased our van in November 2005 and we paid it off in December 2008. That's three years! Think about taking out a car loan. Generally people take them out for five years (like we had) because that's all the monthly payment they can afford.

I shared with my sister about the blessing of paying our van off early and do you know what she said? "Can you do that?" Again this goes to show the mindset that is so easy to remain in, when we become a slave to money. God's specific words are that the borrower is a slave to the lender (Proverbs 22:7b HCSB). It is not His plan for us to have a loan for everything that we buy. Sometimes His plan is for us not to buy!! The pull of the world is so strong. We see what others have and translate what they have into a "need" for us. We need new carpet. We need a bedroom set. We need a vacation.

God says that He provides for our needs (Philippians 4:19). The mistake that I regularly make is not going to Him first. If He already knows what I am in need of, why not ask Him for it? Think about it—He is aware of the time frame for my need, the urgency of my need, and the resources required to meet my need. But rarely would I go to God in prayer for my needs. Instead I would put myself in His place and provide by my own means.

However, there are even times when we may have the money to purchase something and He still wants to give it to us for free. We have been given restaurant gift cards, clothing, amusement park tickets, and groceries, all without asking God for these things. Now imagine what can happen when we have the faith to pray to God, trusting that He will supply what we need. There's some serious power in that.

God had done the impossible. He took $44,000 in debt and paid it off to His glory! Not because we deserved it, but because He could do it. Let me encourage you that what He did for me, He will do for you.

CHAPTER 10

BUYING AND BLESSING

OUR DEBT is paid off!

A load is lifted. We had lived frugally for nearly two years and had become very accustomed to doing so. Once the debt was paid off, we had set some additional goals to waterproof our boat. (Remember Chapter 8?)

I shared earlier about the $1,000 emergency savings account and its purpose in taking care of the unexpected things that come about in life. Well, you and I both know of people who have had an issue so huge happen that $1,000 would not even touch it. For example, as we were going through this time of transforming our finances, if I or Ross had lost our job, we would not have been able to cover our monthly living expenses. Therefore, our next goal was to save three months of our living expenses in the bank. In our case this was $10,000. Saving this money would help us to guard even more so against the unexpected. This was the heat pump money that we should have had but didn't a few years earlier. It seemed like an impossible amount of money to save, but so did $1,000 until we did it. Besides, we had just paid off $44,000 in debt. So we were basically doing what we did before only: 1) we didn't need as much money, and 2) we got to keep the money instead of paying it to someone!

It took us just under a year to fully fund our emergency savings account. We could have done it faster,

Chapter 10 Buying and Blessing

but one of the ventures that we took on, in addition to saving, was learning how to spend money again.

After our debts had been paid off, we made the decision together to purchase some things that were not necessities, but conveniences. If you are anything like us, you will find that after years of saving every dime you can get your hands on, spending is not an automatic reflex.

Because of the focus we had put on saving, spending almost felt sinful! Especially spending money for something that was not a need! But as I mentioned earlier, we made the decision together (unlike in our previous life) to purchase specific items that our family desired. Ross and I met together and came up with a list of about ten items that we wanted. Separately, we put those items in order of priority. Then we came together with our numbered list and gave our proposals as to why we listed the items in the particular order that we did. Once this was done, we reasoned together to agree on an order in which we would pursue purchasing these items. Unlike previously, we approached our spending in unity and with wisdom.

One of the first items that we had decided to purchase was a newer computer as the old one was purchased over ten years ago. The first thing we did was look at <u>Consumer Reports</u> in order to learn more about computers and to find out the best one to buy for what we needed. After deciding on a computer, we looked for the best deals, checking our warehouse club and employee discounts provided through work.

Then we **saved** the money for the computer. Without the previous debts that we owed, each month we had a substantial amount of money that we were able to allot towards the purchase of the computer. What a change from using the credit card! It didn't take long at all to save the money and have a brand new, **paid-for** computer on our desk.

I stated that the computer was one of the first items we pursued. Along with that purchase, we also began investing. Each of us had a retirement account through our employers. Through the recommendations of books that we read, we set a goal of investing 15% of our income. With each monthly budget, some of the extra money that previously went towards debt was placed into our investment account. I will readily admit that I am not well-versed on the topic of investing. But there are some references listed at the end of the book for sources on the topic that were helpful to us.

As I write to you now, we are about half way through completing the purchases from our list. Partly because after the first five items, we have been too busy to put the time into pursuing these purchases and partly because we are not ready yet to invest the money into some of the items that are not needs. God has even shown us that some of the items He will give to us.

One of the items at the top of our list was a set of bunk beds for our boys. They share a room and it was becoming fairly crowded with all of their stuff and two beds. I was sharing one day at work about looking to buy the beds for our kids and my co-worker, Kathy, told me that she had a bunk bed in her basement that her son was no longer using. When I asked her how much she wanted for it, guess what she told me? Nothing! We got a set of sturdy, solid wood bunk beds for absolutely nothing! I truly believe that God can give us **all** of the items on our list for nothing. Do you believe?

I shared with you some of the things we've done for our family now that there is extra money. But I haven't shared with you my favorite thing to do with it. I love to give to others.

Giving feels so good. Yes, I feel good when I get something from someone (like the bunk beds). But nothing on this earth can compare with the feeling of being able to give something to someone that they want or need. Since we no longer live to make ends meet, we can provide for others. I love being able to go out for a meal with someone and pay for them and me both. It is a joy when our church has a need where the congregation is asked to give and we can contribute to this need rather than being angry that we were asked to give. Offering to pay for a tire for my mom's car is not a burden but a blessing because there is not an obligation on her to pay me back. God has shown me clearly by paying off our debts, that our money is His money, so I thoroughly enjoy spending His money the way that He would—helping others. It doesn't get any better than that!

Personal Finances Personal Freedom

CHAPTER 11

PASSING IT ON

AS PARENTS we want the best for our children. Certainly there are a handful of exceptions of parents that have issues and problems such that this is not the case. But I believe I can safely say that, generally, we as parents want our kids to be, as I've heard it said many times, "better off than I was."

I have come to realize in my own life and from the encounters I have had with others that many people were never taught as children how to handle money. Generally, birthday and Christmas money is quickly spent on a toy or other gift of the child's choosing, or well-meaning parents take the money, unbeknownst to the child, and place it into the child's savings account. Now, don't get me wrong, there is nothing wrong with spending and saving gift money. But when a child who is old enough to understand is left out of the process, it truly is a shame. Any encounter that a child has with money is an opportunity to learn about how to handle it properly. When they can develop an appreciation and an understanding for money matters at a young age, it sets them on course to be responsible with God's resources for a lifetime.

Ross and I began teaching our children about money at an early age—when our youngest were about three and four. At this age they began receiving an allowance, not "just because," but for chores they would do in our

Chapter 11 Passing It On

home. This decision was made even before we got on track with our own finances; as I shared earlier, we always want our kids to be better off than we were.

Our kids receive an allowance every week in dollars that equal the age that they are. This is something they can easily relate to and remember. When they were younger, we would set out their money on the table and ask,

"How old are you?"

"Three," they would answer.

"That's right. How many dollars do you get?"

"Three," they would answer.

Relating money to numbers or other concepts that children can understand is extremely helpful. As our children got older, they became aware of the different coins as they began to learn about money in school. It was amazing to see the connection click between the math they were learning about at school and the money they were handling at home. When they began to learn about percentages, we would show them how many of each of the different coins (penny, nickel, dime and quarter) made up a dollar. Of even greater importance, learning percentages gave them an understanding of the tithe.

Tithing has always been a staple in our home. This is only because of God. It has nothing to do with how "good" we are. He has placed the value of tithing in our hearts so we can take no credit for it whatsoever. It comes easy to us. To help you understand what I am trying to say, let me give you a true-to-life illustration.

There was a woman in our church in need of a kidney. Her name is Linda. For various reasons her children and other family members were unable or advised not to donate the organ to her. Without a thought, a member of our church tried to donate a kidney to her but was unable to do so. Therefore the need for an organ for Linda was brought before our church. I thought to myself (as did eight other people), "A kidney? No problem. I'd love to be able to help." I began the process of screening to be a living donor on April 5, 2002, and on July 9, 2002, Linda received my left kidney. Now, certainly that is the condensed version of the story and I would be remiss if I did not share with you that Linda is thriving in her new life. My point in sharing this story is that just like donating a kidney, in my eyes, was a no-brainer; tithing to me is also a no-brainer. I just do it. You know from what I shared that the money was not flowing to the point that tithing was not a sacrifice—in fact, it has been most of our married life. But God put something in us where we know that not tithing is not an option.

So when it came to our kids, we knew that it was necessary for them to learn this principle early in life. We wanted it to come as naturally for them as it had for us. They would participate in the process by selecting where they wanted their tithe to go (general offering or Pastor's love offering), then by putting their money in the envelope and placing it in the offering basket. Doing leads to developing. By **doing** the necessary steps to give their tithe we were **developing** in them the routine

Chapter 11 Passing It On

of giving. Tithing then becomes a natural part of what they do and makes up who they are.

I don't want my children to even have a sense of "missing" this portion of their money. I want them, from the time that they are little, to consider it God's money and therefore not even theirs to be missed—it never belonged to them. Not to be callous about it, but I look at my tithes and offerings as bills. We all can identify with the fact that bills must be paid. On our monthly spreadsheet of expenses, the tithes and offerings are listed right on there. Yes, they are at the top, but they are on there nonetheless along with a whole lot of other mandatory payments.

Yes, the tithe is to be holy and set apart (Leviticus 27:30), but isn't that how we treat our rent money? When it comes to paying the rent we'll do what we have to do to gather up that money and pay because we don't want to be evicted. I dare say that for most people, when they do tithe, it is not with the same "reverence" with which they pay their rent or mortgage. The tithe has been reduced to a tip as my pastor would say. People give to God what they can, if they can and when they can. What reverence is there in that? So before you tell me that putting tithes and offerings on my list of bills is hypocritical, tell me—where is tithing on your list?

Let's turn our focus back to the kids. Once they have set aside their tithe, we have them divide the money left over into two piles—saving and spending. They put half into one and half into the other. Before the age of three years old, all of the money after the tithe went into savings. Just think, when children are young it is the only time that they will easily be able to put away 100% of what they receive. All of the birthday, holiday and "just because" money can be put away directly into the bank without resistance from your child because at this age they have no true concept of money. Take advantage of this time! I say that both jokingly and seriously. Never again will there be a time when you can do what you want with your child's money without hearing complaints! But more seriously, this will start off your child's little nest egg and the routine of saving for a lifetime.

We could simply tell our children that **all** of the money they get goes into savings while they are under our care. However, doing this takes away many opportunities to learn about how money is handled. For example, whenever they go to a friend's birthday party, we expect them to buy the gift. Some of the preparations they need to make to buy that gift include:

- Finding out how much money they have available to spend
- Determining how much the gift the friend wants costs
- Doing some research to find out where to get the gift at the best price

The last step is usually done with the help of mommy and daddy, but the other steps our two older kids can tackle alone. All three of our kids keep a ledger which consists of a small memo pad with three columns: one

Chapter 11 Passing It On

for the date, one for the transaction, and one for the balance. To accomplish step number one, they can look at the balance on the spending side of the memo pad to see how much is in their piggy bank. For step number two, they will talk to the friend and find out what kinds of things he or she likes. Sometimes they know already. Lastly, we will talk with them about what stores we might want to go to for the best price, whether there is a sale somewhere or a coupon we can clip.

Talking about these things with them becomes a part of normal, everyday conversation. We don't keep it a secret when mommy and daddy cannot afford something—we just tell them outright that we don't have the money for XYZ or we don't want to pay the money that XYZ costs. Saying "no" is not a problem for us because saying "yes" is what got us into trouble in the first place. We don't feel like we're depriving our children, we feel like we're inspiring them to be responsible with the money that God gives them. Good parents say "no" while their children are still young and under their care so that they can handle hearing "no" when they are out in the world and away from the nest.

Using their own money to purchase things has taught our children patience. Oftentimes they have wanted things that they did not have enough money to buy. In this case they would need to keep saving their weekly allowance until they had enough money to make the big purchase. Inevitably they would see other things that they wanted during this time, but would need to dismiss those other temptations for what they had their hearts set on in the first place. This is just like life as an adult. Ladies, that purse looks good and it would only set you back twenty dollars. But if we fall for the purse, we'll fall for the matching pair of shoes too, right? In the same way if our kids can learn about saving towards a goal, it provides them with a wonderful lesson on perseverance in both finances and other areas of their future lives.

I remember being in high school and having so much anxiety over clothing. It was all about wearing the right brands, even the songs on the radio talked about a certain brand of jeans that was right to wear. As a teen I would fret over being a fashion misfit in the midst of my friends. Looking back I see how unimportant clothes truly were during my schooling, but it doesn't mean that those feelings that I had were not real for me.

As parents, Ross and I try to put as little emphasis on brands as possible. When we do get name brands for our kids, it is either at a really good price or they are hand-me-downs. I refuse to pay so much money for something that, 1) is not going to give my child success, and 2) that my child is going to grow out of in six months. With three children in our home, hand-me-downs have been a way of life. I have to laugh sometimes when moms cautiously approach me and say, "I'm not sure if you take used clothes or not but my son has outgrown these and..."—the words are barely out of their mouth and I'm grabbing the bag out of their hands because I will take used clothes in a heartbeat. The cutest thing is that my kids love having these "new" clothes to wear.

Chapter 11 Passing It On

When people compliment them on their clothes, they even recite to them what friend we got them from.

Yard sales are another good source for kids' clothes. (Don't get me started on yard sales—I love them!) Now I know that this stage of my kids loving to wear other kids' clothing is likely a temporary thing. Surely when they get older, they may want their own new clothes to buy and wear. But when they are older, they will also have jobs and their own money to spend on these must-have clothes. Until then, I will revel in their appreciation of hand-me-downs!

It is a blessing to see our children understanding what we are teaching them about money. I believe that my daughter, Morgan, is going to be a true spendthrift. When we go to yard sales, she haggles a price and will say no to something if it's not what she wants to pay for it—truly a girl after my own heart. It is not unusual to hear the words, "I can't believe their charging such-and-such dollars for this" come out of her mouth. It is clear that she gets it and has learned about the value of money.

Our children watched us as we went through the process of getting out of debt. We shared with them as different items were paid off and we let them know about certain limitations that we had set. I don't believe they felt deprived, because we didn't act deprived. God provided for us mightily the entire time and still allowed us to go out, have recreation time, and enjoy our children. There were times that we said "no," but we said "no" before so this was not a shock to them—

just reality. When parents show their children how to tithe, save money, spend money responsibly, buy with cash, and use little to no credit, they prepare them to be financially sound adults later in life.

Epilogue

Personal Freedom

These days I feel like I am living a different life. Not only do I feel free to spend money, but I also feel free not to spend it. In my former life I felt obligated to get what everyone else had. Now I know that many people don't truly own what they have—they're still paying for it!

Freedom for me has meant being able to leave my job and be home for my family. Freedom is being able to give money to someone and not need it back to meet my own needs. Freedom is being able to share my victory through this book and know that God can use it to change your life.

I shared with you in Chapter 5 that I now have a new definition for the term "money factor." Remember, I used to say that it is the underlying realization that finances affect and, in many cases, limit that which you desire for your lifestyle. Today I declare that the money factor is the freedom that you have to control your personal finances instead of letting them control you. The money factor means planning out how your money will be best spent before you have even received it. This is the essence of being a good steward.

May God bless you in your Personal Finances to experience Personal Freedom.

Recommended Reading

Bach, David, *Smart Couples Finish Rich*, New York: Broadway Books, 2001.

Bach, David, *Smart Women Finish Rich*, New York: Broadway Books, 1999.

Ford, Justin, *Seeds of Wealth*, Baltimore: Seeds of Wealth, LLC, 2005.

Ramsey, Dave, *The Total Money Makeover: A Proven Plan for Financial Fitness*, Tennessee: Thomas Nelson, Inc., 2003.

Singletary, Michelle, *Your Money and Your Man: How You and Prince Charming Can Spend Well and Live Rich*, New York: Ballantine Books, 2007.

Soaries, DeForest B., Jr., *dfree: Breaking Free from Financial Slavery*, Michigan: Zondervan, 2011.

Stanley, Thomas. J., and Danko, William D., *The Millionaire Next Door: The Surprising Secrets of America's Wealthy*, Georgia: Longstreet Press, 1996.

PERSONAL FINANCES PERSONAL FREEDOM

is available at:

olivepresspublisher.com

amazon.com

barnesandnoble.com

and other websites.

The E-book is available at:

amazon.com

Book stores and book distributors may obtain this book through:

Ingram Book Company

or by e-mailing

olivepressbooks@gmail.com

CPSIA information can be obtained
at www.ICGtesting.com
Printed in the USA
BVHW070225160219
540405BV00001B/7/P